ALLAH THE MAKER SERIES

*The Islamic Foundation would like to gratefully acknowledge the efforts of
brother Anwar Cara for developing the* ALLAH THE MAKER SERIES
*concept, sister Fatima M. D'Oyen for editing, Mr. E. R. Fox for copy
editing and proofreading, and Dr. M. Manazir Ahsan and
Dr. Kidwai for their general encouragement and support.*

MUSLIM CHILDREN'S LIBRARY

ANIMALS
Author: Farah Sardar
Illustrator: Vinay Ahluwalia (Bhagirti Art Studio, New Delhi)

Published by
The Islamic Foundation, Markfield Conference Centre, Ratby Lane,
Markfield, Leicester LE67 9RN, United Kingdom
Tel: (01530) 244944 Fax: (01530) 244946 E-Mail: i-foundation@islamic-foundation.org.uk

Quran House, PO Box 30611, Nairobi, Kenya

PMB 3193, Kano, Nigeria

Printed by Renault Printing Co. Ltd., Birmingham, England B44 8BS

ALLAH THE MAKER SERIES

ANIMALS

by FARAH SARDAR

illustrated by VINAY AHLUWALIA

THE ISLAMIC FOUNDATION

Allah made butterflies
With two bright wings

Allah made birds
That fly high and sing

Allah made squirrels
Who scurry up trees

Allah made the furry coats
Of busy, buzzing bees

Allah made camels
With great big humps

Allah made elephants
With long, slinky trunks

Allah made hippos
Who wallow in lakes

Allah made slithery,
Slippery snakes!

Allah made frogs
That spring with a leap

Allah made ducks
With two webbed feet

Allah made fish that
Swim deep in the seas

Allah made monkeys that
Swing high from the trees

Allah made polar bears
To live in snow and ice

Allah made zebras
With zig-zag stripes

Allah made giraffes
With long, thin necks

Allah made hens
With beaks to peck

Allah made tortoises
With homes on their backs

Allah made beetles
With coats shiny black

Allah made cats
With eyes so bright

Allah made owls
That hoot at night:
Who? Who?
Allah - Hoo!

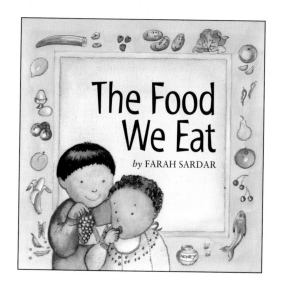

Also available in this series

The Food We Eat
by FARAH SARDAR
illustrated by ASIYA CLARKE

A lively and entertaining account,
capturing the tastes, textures and
infinite variety of food provided by Allah

ALLAH GAVE ME TWO EYES TO SEE (*by* F. D'Oyen)

THANK YOU, O ALLAH (*compiled by* F. D'Oyen)